COFFEE & CONTEMPLATION
–a taste of empowerment–

MALIK MUHAMMAD

First published in Great Britain in 2020
by Rhodium Publishing.

Photography: Zuzana Dahamshy

Cover Design: Yasmin Flemming

Copy Editor: Pardeep Sall

ISBN: 978-1-8381275-0-3

COFFEE & CONTEMPLATION
– a taste of empowerment –

TABLE OF CONTENTS

Stardust to stardust, we are ancient souls
Studies prove we are made of old
Formed in stars we shine as light
To live each day and rest each night.

The conscious mind lays behind the eyes
Steering our body through passing time
Reality is, we build who we are
No limits on how you set each bar.

Learn everyday what is right for yourself
Create your dreams, with no negative dwell
Surround yourself with positive ties
That link in a circle, empowering life.

Think of those faces who tell you their worth
A silent leader who roams through this earth
Passion in voice that everyone breathes
A soul that is dancing through years of belief.

Belief is a state that is simple and clear
So believe in yourself – conquer failure and fear
Your body, your strength is more than enough
For any achievement you give the right love.

Read a book that enlightens your day
Listen to wisdom that's shying away

Write out your thoughts and scribble the lands
Bring words to life in the palm of your hands.

For I shall live 100 years
and make of it what you will.

–Hannah Elizabeth Philpot

WHY THIS TITLE?

This book is neither about coffee nor is it just for coffee lovers. The purpose of this book is to help you see the personal benefit of creating moments to think about your special life, plan for the future and truly appreciate the present.

The chapters will encourage you to come off line and get in line with your mind. The exercises will naturally encourage you to develop the ritual of prioritising time for yourself each day.

The thoughts are expressed in ways that will challenge how you think. Reading this book will give you the tools to schedule the time to have a few moments for yourself each day.

Those moments may be in the shower, on the way to school, over lunch, before bed, with your favourite drink or experiencing a cup of coffee.

Some of my special moments are over coffee, hence, the title. A coffee moment is a sacred experience. It is a ritual that creates personal time and allows me to engage in meaningful conversation, solve problems, think or simply be present.

It's much more meaningful than a hot beverage that keeps me awake. So much more than something I need in the morning to function effectively or a liquid habit that helps me focus.

Coffee represents sweet indulgence of the highest calibre through engaging with a drink that feels good, tastes sublime and encourages elevated thinking.

I appreciate the entire coffee experience. You may not. It doesn't matter. What matters is that you train yourself to think objectively and see things from different perspectives before coming to informed conclusions.

Making progress in this life requires strategic thinking and consistent actions. It is the effective cultivation of these strategies that empower you to be the best version of yourself.

Welcome to Coffee & Contemplation
—a taste of empowerment—

1. CULTIVATING YOUR VISION

Have you ever wasted a day? Have you ever spent way too much time on social media? If so, you have lost precious time that could have been used to do something for yourself.

The degree to which we allow things, people and circumstances to distract us is the degree to which we move further away from our visions, missions and aims.

This life is neither a joke nor a dress rehearsal. Seconds become minutes, minutes become hours, hours become days, days become weeks, weeks become months and months become years.

None of these time spans can be recreated once they are experienced. A few seconds of your life have gone in the time you have read these words. (You have invested the time wisely so please read on). Everything happens right now in the present so it makes sense to use your time as productively as possible.

You are fallible not flawed. Yes - there have been a few errors in judgment along the way. You could probably have done a few things differently.

There may even have been a few missed opportunities. No - you are not the devil incarnate. You are neither cursed nor is your life doomed to failure. There is a good life in front of you.

It is time to get what's yours. This is the moment and the time and the era to cultivate your vision. The trajectory of your life may have taken a certain direction that you did not anticipate. Is this how you want your life story to end? What's stopping you from living your best life? Who or what is distracting you?

The greatest distractor is the enemy within you and battling with the negative, doubtful, quiet voice in yourself can be an ongoing reality. Such is the yin and yang of this experience called life. Learning the lessons from each life experience doesn't mean living in the Himalayas or the Blue Mountains of Jamaica, being vegan, abstaining from sex, wearing sackcloth & ashes and chanting for 40 days without food or human contact.

Learning from the lessons in your life means being able to change your behaviour for the better while you are dealing with every day realities like paying bills, doing school runs, handling difficult family members, studying etc.

Time keeps moving even when we are tempted to stand still. Ready or not, be assured that life comes at you and it keeps coming until you transcend this physical experience.
This is why you benefit from respecting your time and investing it wisely.

Watching 5 hours of entertaining late night television can feel real good. It's not so good when you have to rise early in the morning for an appointment that requires an alert mind.

The extra 30 minute lie-in that occurred because 'I couldn't be bothered to get up' means you rushed to get ready, then dashed to where you had to be, became stressed because you were running late and the rest of the day just ran away.

What was the root cause of your rushing around? It was that unnecessary 30 minute lie-in.

Procrastination is habitual and it develops in small increments. It's seductive because many of us like the path of least resistance. Mediocre people love wasting time, enjoy being busy rather than productive and have an excuse for everything.

It's a hell of a thing when you know deep in your gut that you can do better but you're too afraid to leave your familiar circumstances and people behind.

Sometimes we simply outgrow our circle of friends or finally accept that certain family members are toxic. Loyalty to that which is clearly hurting us will eventually break us.

Do you remember when I asked you if you had ever spent too much time on social media? In this era of positive social media memes and inspirational quotes it is so easy to get an encouraging word about having a positive mental attitude.

The rhetoric abounds on various social media platforms and every Tom, LaShonda or Gertrude can provide an uplifting word via the re-posting of some quote from a celebrity (who probably didn't say or write it in the first place).

The spread of positivity is a good thing and an uplifting word can warm the cockles of the heart in times of anxiety.

The challenge is that actions are needed to activate the words as mere words count for nothing until carried into practice.
The inspiration from quotes must create a call to action within the soul of the reader. This is in the similar way that prayer works if you pray then immediately go to work.

Who do you take more seriously: the person who always says what they are going to do or the person who simply does it?
I am certain it's the person who simply does it.

Talking has its place as do planning, analysing, strategising, researching and so forth. All these processes count for naught until something is done. Action is the main thing.

Keep the main thing as the main thing once you have committed to bringing about your vision. There is a commonly held view in the world of personal development that you need to believe something in order to achieve it.

A belief is anything you hold to be true. You can believe whatever you want. Commitment is what truly matters.

We will explore the primary benefits of being committed in Chapter 4: Stickability.

Belief is overrated.
Believing you can fly will not make you fly but taking flying lessons will improve your options. Do you really think the universe won't test you to see how much you really want what you say you want?

Be prepared to face obstacles, go through hell and handle disappointment because that is how you qualify yourself and develop character in order to claim what you desire.

Will you always get what you desire even after all the pain and sacrifice? No.
Is it still worth going through all that? Yes.
How does that make sense? It makes sense because you grow through what you go through.

You will be emotionally stronger, better prepared and more experienced to handle whatever life throws at you the next time.

Maintaining the focus in cultivating your vision is fraught with distractions. Things will happen that can take you off course. Curve balls come in life and on the baseball court. It can be a slow journey bringing your vision to fruition.

The journey / race is not for the swift and impatient. It is only for those who endure to the end.

The mind-set of Mohammed Farah (Mo Farah) after his fall in the 10,000m events at the Rio 2016 Olympics is an appropriate reference point. Farah fell with 16 laps to go, got back up, won the race. He entered the 2016 Olympics as the reigning champion which was enough pressure in and of itself.

Farah is on record as saying that he promised his daughter Rhianna a gold medal and he could not let her down. With all his training and years of preparation he could not anticipate falling. Things were not going according to plan but his focus pulled him through.

He trained his body to deal with whatever happened in that race. He also trained his mind.

He went beyond merely believing he could win.

He was committed to winning even before entering the race and this is why he trained, sacrificed and prepared on all levels over a 4-year period.

His very spirit was in sync with realising his vision. His body and mind functioned in alignment. His body and mind functioned as one unit.

Do you see what we are talking about here?

The time came when you had to leave the comfort of the womb of your mother to be birthed. You inadvertently acknowledge the pain you and your mother experienced when you commemorate that date each year by calling it your 'birthday'.

You have grown, you took some hits / licks in life and you are still here. You have reached further along the scale of your great evolution since birth. You have learned and will keep learning because self-empowerment is an ever unfolding experience.

You become a more resilient person through struggle whether or not you get that which your heart desired.

Let me add a subtle caveat.

Things don't always work according to plan so you must learn to handle disappointment. I am of the opinion that you should approach everything you desire with the full intention of getting what you want.

Don't half step or approach with doubt. Put in the work and expect to get the results. Commit to what you want and be consistent in your sacrifice to achieve it.

This 'grow through what you go through' stuff is not to pacify or patronise you if things go wrong. It is a reminder that things go wrong every once in a while and you have to handle the disappointment that may follow. Things go off key even with the most precise plan.

You can whinge, moan and become deflated or you can reassess, hold a meditation and rise like the mythical phoenix. The choice is yours. You may be thinking "but Malik, you don't understand. Life has been so hard for me. I had no choice". Hold on a little bit, stop right there and don't move a muscle.

There is always a choice.

The decision you make to have no choice is actually a choice within itself.

There is always a choice because you have the free will to make certain decisions about your life given the immediate circumstances.

The clarity and passion you felt in what you just read comes from the core philosophy at the centre of my amazing evolution.

Real recognizes real hence I wrote it, you read it and our intellectual souls are in alignment in this moment. You feel me and I feel you. Stop being afraid of how powerful you are!

If you already know your power then this book will inspire you to keep rising in your power. If you don't know your power then this book is guaranteed to help and positively influence you.

Leaders lead and cowards cower.

Acknowledging your power is not arrogance or false pride. It's straight-up confidence.

*Embracing your personal power is **sine qua non** to breathing life into anything you envision.*

You are taken seriously when you take yourself seriously.

To command respect from others you must first respect yourself.

Notice I said command respect, not demand respect. Respect is generally given to you when you represent yourself as an individual who knows their worth, is comfortable in their own skin and clear about their core values.

Respect flows like the Martha Brae River in Jamaica when people know you are consistent in what you stand for. Respect is offered when your good character speaks for itself.

Demonstrate some inner love by taking yourself seriously and stop joking with your future.

Increase your internal peace by moving on that idea you've had for a while. Step up and move out!

You command respect by being comfortable in who you are. There's no need to define yourself by your title, how much money you earn or what you do for a living.

The first step to receiving genuine respect (as opposed to being liked or being popular) is by embracing your own magnificence and acting accordingly.

Are you puzzled by the way your enemies and detractors are obsessed with you? Do you ever wonder why they are talking about you, slide in your DM's or write negative comments in your timeline? It's because they know you don't give a .... about what they do or think.

They understand that lions don't listen to sheep. They realise that they are not important enough in your life for their opinions to ever matter to you.

They want your life. It hurts them that they are irrelevant, immaterial and inconsequential in your magnificent life. Distractions take you away from the straight path of what you decided to do. Stay in your lane and handle your business one vision at a time.

Be specific about what you want to do.

Take consistent actions and make the necessary sacrifices.

Avoid distractions.

Learn from the lessons in disappointment.

Trust your instincts.

2. CORE PHILOSOPHY

Complaining about your life and making excuses for the way things are is understandable at times. You can equally decide to ease up on the complaining and take the necessary actions to change things for the better. Please join me as we explore how to take these necessary actions through a practical exercise, a few supportive examples and a personal recollection.

One of the benefits of investing in personal empowerment is the clarity you receive about what you stand for. The essence of your core philosophy is based on what you stand for.

This clarity enables you to make fundamental decisions regarding many aspects of your life. The values and practices you uphold will definitely impact the way you function in everyday life. Your core values help you to compromise within certain boundaries - but no further. The line beyond which you will not cross is clearly marked and you are willing to deal with the consequences thereof. The principles that make up the essence of how you live become a personal code of conduct. It is akin to an internal mission statement for your life at this point. It's a culmination of the truths that guide how you function. Here is a simple 4 step exercise to help you establish or reaffirm said truths.

4 STEP VALUE IDENTIFICATION EXERCISE

Duration: 15 minutes quiet time.
Resources required: one sheet of blank paper, a pen and an open mind.
Learning outcome: To clearly identify then list three values that make up your core philosophy.

STEP 1. Think about three values that you would never compromise.
STEP 2. Write down these three values.
STEP 3. Observe the values then list one scenario for each value where you could be seriously tested.
STEP 4. Engage in an honest conversation with yourself as to whether you would compromise your value in each given scenario and, if so, why you would.

The above exercise forces you to really and truly question yourself. Repeat all four steps until you come up with the three values. Identifying what we believe is easier than knowing or even understanding why we believe it.

We are bombarded with thousands of bits of information on a daily basis that compete for our attention. Having basic certainties can often make life easier. Therein lies the danger.

An easier life doesn't necessarily mean a better life. Establishing and understanding what you stand for is another fundamental step to living a life in accordance with your values. If you fail to think critically then others, with ulterior motives, will impose their thoughts about you upon you to the extent that you believe said thoughts are your own.(Read the sentence again if it doesn't make sense). People will mess up your head with foolishness because you fail to think critically.

Children often have a habit of asking ' but why?' when you give them the most basic instruction. It's as if they enjoy disrupting the flow of adult instructions by seeking a deeper explanation.

Take the example of telling a typical child to eat their vegetables when they prefer cereal with dinner. An instruction to 'eat your vegetables, you can't have cereal' may follow with a response 'why?' and when you say 'because it's good for you' you hear another 'but why' because they remember you said that cereal is also 'good for you'.

Child logic concludes that you said vegetables and cereals are 'good for you'.

So they ask for cereal. You say no. They brand you a liar and log that in their fertile minds for future reference. The process of going around the questions about eating the vegetables is similar to how we fail to probe the inner part of ourselves to arrive at what we actually stand for.

Be clear and specific about what you want. Don't send your brain mixed messages. Another extension of the 'eat your vegetables' scenario is that the adult eventually draws on the adult default answer of 'because I said so'. This further complicates the child's mind and still fails to answer the question. The child is just expected to follow without knowing or understanding why.

I accept that most children require discipline. This familiar scenario also highlights how we may be susceptible to being programmed to do as we are told without questioning why. How often have you acted because someone or something in your culture 'told you so'?

Have you functioned without understanding why you believe or do certain things? Ponder on these questions for a moment.

There is an intellectual conflict between the mindsets that uplift and those that restrict our growth. This is an internal battle of the will. Desire feeds the will. The more you desire positivity for yourself, the more you battle to overcome all potential impediments to your self empowerment.

This is another expression of the yin and yang. This is another manifestation of the struggle for balance. As you proceed to give your soul what it needs you will unequivocally define what it means to have a clear reference system / mission statement / core philosophy. Clear guidance (via the soul) makes the physical manifestation (via the body) much more successful and focused and results orientated. Cherish your intelligence.

Established theories in many subject areas were once mocked, ridiculed and even dismissed by the populace before they became generally accepted. We will now look at a brief history of home security systems and drip feed devices in support of my opinion. Home security systems are standard now but when Marie and Albert Van Brittan Brown filed their patent application in August 1966, it was genuinely the first of its kind.

It was for an audio and video security system for a house under the control of the occupant thereof. Bessie Blount invented an electric self-feeding device that delivered food via a tube in very small quantities. The morsels of food were fed into a mouthpiece that could be used whether someone was lying down or sitting up.

Why is this relevant? The device was to help improve the quality of life of less physically abled persons. He/she would bite on the tube that would then signal a machine to release the next morsel. Blount was unable to get it patented and gave it to France. In 1951 she patented the portable receptacle support that was designed to help people to feed themselves.

*It was the erudite social commentator Nasir 'Nas' Jones who opined **"people fear what they do not understand; hate what they can't conquer".***

The backstory of most inventors or progressive thinkers is oft as amazing as the high quality of their inventions or ideas. Groupthink is real. The willingness to express an alternative view or develop a fresh perspective on established theories can be daunting; yet, such actions are necessary for human development.

Let's take a look at the longstanding passive-aggressive antagonism between people of faith.

Much lip service is paid to the oneness of faith and a wide range of ecumenical services /outreach programmes pay fleeting homage to how well the different expressions of spiritual systems appear to work together.

A little deeper probing of this surface unity reveals that there will never be a genuine acceptance because each religion believes it has 'the truth'. The irony is that the theological disagreements in religion actually perpetuate division.

There is also money and bragging rights in the perceived truth. People follow these truths because they have been conditioned to accept them as the truth.

I find it ironic that these very nuanced yet deeply held theological disagreements are simply different ways of saying the same thing based on culture, language, geographic location and other influences.

The agnostic who dares to question the basis of said inconsistencies is then cast aside by said people of faith for not subscribing to the overall doctrine of a supreme being – as they understand it.

This is the same doctrine that even they, as people of faith, do not agree upon by the way. It would be simpler to respect the different understandings of the oneness in creation in the same way that there is one sun with many rays that gives light wherever you are in this world.

There is only one sun that shines over the entire earth. Whoever or whatever one credits for this blessing is, therefore, irrelevant. The sun simply shines.

"When the rain falls, it don't fall on one man house"
–Bob Marley, So Much Things To Say.

The sun shines, the rains fall and the seasons change despite our belief systems. The sun still executes its natural function as a life-giving expression in our magnificent universe. The sun shines and brings life.

The higher principle of appreciating the blessing of the sun is often lost in the doctrinal minutiae as to whose God deserves the credit. Exposure to other points of view truly nourishes the mind. This exposure can challenge your ideas but it will help you to clearly identify what you represent as an individual.

Trust your intelligence. Stand firm in what you feel once you have established your way of seeing the world. Have the courage to espouse your point of view as you hold firm to what you see in your mind.

It's time we wrapped up this chapter so please accept my thanks for doing the value identification exercise and entertaining my perspectives thus far.

I'll share my final thoughts on core philosophy by tapping a little into my teenage years by way of personal recollection.

My second year of high school education in Jamaica created an experience that still has an indelible impact on what I now understand to be part of my core philosophy.

Our innovative literature teacher came in with a ghetto blaster and cassette tape. Ghetto blaster is the common name for a large portable radio and cassette or CD player. Cassette tape is an analog magnetic tape recording format for audio recording or playback. Our literature teacher – Ms.Campbell – gently placed the items on her desk in front of our eager collective gaze. She informed us that Sonia Sanchez, Chinua Achebe, Shakespeare, Braithwaite, Chaucer, Baldwin, Jane Austin et al. ought to be contextualised and understood.

She suggested that literary expressions from our collective experience in Jamaica were a valid, yet often overlooked, part of the global literary landscape.

She then pressed the 'play' button on the ghetto blaster and I heard poetry and perspectives that filled my soul with pride, my intellect with creative awareness and my vision of the future with clear spiritual focus.

The grand cadence of what I heard next has influenced my ability to later comprehend what Stephen R. Covey refers to as interdependence being a higher value than independence.

It has positively affected my understanding of spirituality, world affairs and my place in the global stratosphere.

It also taught me what it means to be authentic.

The clarity of reasoning and the articulation of critical thinking exemplified in the poetry has had a major impact on how I see life.

I recall the public scorn, general mockery and open vilification that was associated with such elevated thinking. The musings of the great soul that came forth from that ghetto blaster have stood the test of time. When you are clear about your core philosophy, you withstand the stormy sea of misinformed opinions, petty platitudes and cyclical whims.

You are anchored in this sea because you are clear about what you stand for. You know your non-negotiable points.

You function within specific boundaries. You are confident about how far you will go in a given situation and know the point beyond which you will never compromise.

There is unspeakable joy in this personal confidence and unlimited fulfilment within your soul. You live in the abundance of your power.

You impact generations unborn and rotate from a higher axis of self-empowerment.

You validate yourself rather than seek the acceptance or constant approval of others.

We are talking about core philosophy. Core may be defined as a part of something that is central to its existence. Other words for core are primary, essential or fundamental. Philosophy is a noun rooted in the Latin term philosophia which is a transliteration of two Greek rooted words: Philo (love) and Sophos (wisdom). It is beneficial to identify the self- loving wisdom that guides your behaviour. This body of wisdom is as clear as it is organic. Here are some questions you may ask yourself to help you identify your core philosophy:

What is my mission statement?
What principles guide my life right now?
How do I decide what to do in conflicting situations?

Create the time to ponder on these questions because they will enable you to get clarity and continue to live your best life.

"Very little is needed to make a happy life. It is all within in your way of thinking. You have the power over your mind – not outside events. Realize this and you will find strength. Everything we hear is an opinion, not a fact. Everything we see is a perception, not the truth".

–Marcus Aurelius

That high school English Literature class experience challenged how I thought and opened my teenage mind to other perspectives in the intellectual realm. Ms. Campbell prompted me to wonder why I believed and thought the way I believed and thought.

Great progressive minds in academia should be honoured and cherished at all levels. I honour all teachers and all in education in this moment.

Ms Marcia Hylton is the brilliant academic who shaped my mind. She will forever be the primary intellectual and literary influence in my life. Her expression of divine femininity is simply beautiful in its manifestation.

My high school English and literature class served as an introduction to critical thinking, not an attempt at persuasion or indoctrination. My mind smiles at the recollection even now.

The transformational power of the audio content of that 90 minute JVC cassette tape in the grey & black twin speaker ghetto blaster still reverberates in my soul and stokes the fire of self- empowerment in every cell of my being.

What did I hear?

I heard an authentic expression that spoke to the richness of a cultural and spiritual reality.

I heard a silent narrative assuring me that it was ok to understand, accept and be my true self.

*I heard the creatively intelligent reasoning of the profound Jamaican poet, respected Rastafarian and legendary radio host of **The Cutting Edge** and **Stepping Razor**.*

I heard the voice and spirit of Mutabaruka.

3. ACHIEVE MORE TOGETHER

Slipknot. Mint Condition. U2. The Roots. The Rolling Stones. Earth, Wind & Fire. The Who. Chronixx and The Zinc Fence Band. Queen. Motley Crüe. Third World. Black Sabbath. Steve Rubell and Ian Schrager or Warren Buffett and Charlie Munger – a different kind of music based on the rhythm of making money together.

Let me explain what this chapter is all about lest you think it's merely about a list of musical groups and successful business partnerships.

It is a list of musical groups and successful business friendships – but there is a rationale behind the listing. All the groups have long standing success in the music industry. All have sold millions of records and won numerous awards. One of the secrets of their success is that they all have deeply rooted friendships with some even going back to childhood.

The Buffett & Munger connection is legendary both as a friendship and a business relationship. Elements of this were also typical of the Rubell and Schrager connection.

The musical groups and business relationships worked because they operated as teams. Their skillsets complimented each other in pursuit of a common objective. They didn't do it alone. They cannot claim they were 'self- made'.

The bands understood the value of working together and embracing individual skillsets to create timeless music. They were also able to provide for themselves and their families based on the strength of such collaborative thinking. How can this be attributed to doing it alone?

The business partnerships were formed out of mutual respect for and genuine reliance on the ability of each partner to produce specific results. They brought something to the table of progress whether as musicians or as business people.

You may have realised by now that the notion of being 'self- made' has never sat well with me.

The term is an irrational, narcissistic conclusion. Being 'self-made' implies that one received little or no help to be successful in life.

The premise is that you pushed yourself without inheriting the proverbial silver spoon (or family money) to help you get where you are in life.

I get that, but it's not the same as having no support to be the success that you are. We have all had some encouragement. We have all had people on our side doing little things to meet our everyday needs. To be 'self-made' is, therefore, bullshit.

We have all had people who believed in us enough to lend us a helping hand. In this wider sense (like the groups listed at the start of this chapter) we too have had our own band at various times in our lives. The groups / partnerships listed above understood the value of collectively working together to be successful. Their closeness is linked to their success. Their creativity kept them relevant to their fan base despite changes in technology and music trends over the years. They love what they do and love doing it together, hence, the musical giants that they will always be in the annals of recording history.

Think of any music you love. Now look at your favourite group. If they have been around for a reasonably long time you'll find that what you just read also applies to them.

The reality of working together has its ups and downs. Humans can be challenging. Some of the challenges to team work are:

1. Cultural indoctrination against working with others.
2. Lack of appropriate skill set / experience.
3. Ego. Feeling that you are the best knower about how everything should be done.
4. Allowing short-term gratification to overshadow the long-term vision.

Can you imagine the chaos that would ensue if your lungs tried to do what your heart does? The common denominator is that they are both organs in your body yet they have differentiated by their specific functions. All is well once each is allowed to do what they do best and stay in their lane of expertise. All things being equal, the heart and the lungs do their best work according to their areas of speciality to support the overall wellbeing of the body.

This also applies with a successful musical band. Although you can achieve a lot on your own, there is so much more that you will accomplish by joining with likeminded people who share a common vision.

The key point here is the common vision. All parties need to be on the same page, singing a complementary melody, be in harmony with each other, in sync with the same rhythm.

The vision must be effectively communicated to and shared by all parties. The collaboration must function productively.

The roles are equally important even though some roles may receive a higher profile than others, e.g. the adulation received by the lead singer in a band.

The lead singer in a group serves as the front person and for the purpose of this conversation we'll look at Irish rock gods U2.
Lead singer Bono (Paul David Hewson) has alluded to the fact that U2 were a band even before they played well. The Edge (David Howell Evans), Adam Charles Clayton and Lawrence 'Larry' Mullen have a bond that transcends the music they create.

This foundation produced the template for the songs they create together and the global popularity of their sound. This lies at the heart of why they are able to excel.

Do you have a favourite group who have been around for a while? You will see that they too share a strong bond.

The reason for using music groups as an empowerment reference point is to demonstrate that everyday examples are right in front of us. The examples become clear once we prepare ourselves to receive them.

There is also much value in broadening our frames of reference regarding sources of inspiration and challenge some of the philosophies we have been programmed to believe from birth.
Enough about bands.

Great individuals have a way of making us feel good at the mere mention of their names. This applies even if they have transcended this life.
Have you seen the genuine reaction of someone who loves Fay Ellington, Aung San Suu Kyi, Kim Kardashian (or any Kardashian), Nikki Yeoh, Neil deGrasse Tyson, Sadhguru Jaqqi Vasudev, Koffee, Black Thought, Asha Bhosle, Skepta, Megan Thee Stallion, Sheldon Edwards, DVF, Keyon Harrold or SherryAnn Dixon?

There is a devotion to people like this that cannot be logically explained. Logic doesn't always apply when you are deeply touched by the display of someone's gift.

It's not supposed to make logical sense because how you feel transcends logic. It simply connects with your soul and that cannot always be justified through reasoning. It's real and you love the way it makes you feel.

Empowerment involves working with qualified people who share and add value in the cultivation of said vision.

Empowerment includes the ability to understand that you cannot do it alone. The super groups we discussed earlier know this and this is part of the reason they are icons. The individuals we referred to also get this concept. It is a common trait in any truly successful business or ground breaking venture

You can and will do many things based on your own passion and commitment, however, more is done and greater things will be accomplished with the help of the right people – and yes, it is that simple. Individuality is often prided in western societies.
We casually hear about the survival of the fittest, pulling yourself up by the bootstraps, working hard to reach the top of your profession, never quitting, obliterating the competition at all costs and prioritizing money over everything.

This perspective has also penetrated eastern societies through media, globalisation and the gradual denigration of cultural norms. The oversimplification of West is bad / East is good (or vice versa) is not what I am saying.

What I am saying is that things aren't always cut and dry. This or that. There are nuances and contexts to consider because human beings are complex creatures that rely on socialisation and group interaction.

The premise is that we are constantly exposed to the idea that we can do things on our own when the irony is that this is a limiting belief. It does more harm than good.

It breeds arrogance instead of confidence and fans the flames of low self-esteem with self-centeredness. Three of the primary benefits of working with the right people are:

1. The job gets done in less time.
2. Diverse skills and experiences create effective strategies
3. You grow on a personal level through interdependence.

Replacing 'me' with 'we' gets better results in a shorter time and all contributors grow exponentially from the collaborative experience.

Being secure within yourself makes you more willing to collaborate with others and see the value in their gifts.

Feeling secure starts with understanding how special you are in this world. Understanding your value leads to identifying the gifts and abilities that you possess.

Operating from this place of personal abundance raises your self-confidence to the point where you genuinely celebrate the progress of other people. Beware the begrudging, bad-minded and envious individuals who feign happiness for your achievements yet covertly seek your demise.

I spend time around the people that inspire me
-Talib Kweli

Have you ever been in an organisation or group that lost its effectiveness over time? You may not have been in such an organisation but have you read of such a group in ancient or modern history?

I guarantee you that somewhere in the history of that group there was a clash of egos rooted in personal insecurity that led to the inevitable demise of said group.

('Demise' may be a tad theatrical, so let's just say there were major problems).

Positions and titles mean more to the insecure than one can ever imagine. The lowly titled roles that receive no publicity are as important as the high profile positions that get all the publicity. Your valid contribution to the collective vision is all that matters.

This importance is not based on profile, longevity or some other perceived advantage. It is based on playing your part in the bigger picture and that bigger picture is the manifestation of the collective vision.

The fulfilment of each role is critical to the overall success. Understanding this is how we achieve more together. Working together requires clear and effective communication by using whatever medium works best.

Encouragement to collaborate may even come via social media platforms often full of inspirational memes or quotes intended to uplift your spirit. We delve into this in Chapter 7:
When memes aren't enough.

Some such memes make sense whilst others may be dismissed as annoying platitudes that infuriate rather that elevate your consciousness. Even a traditional method of communication known as actually speaking with someone can be impacted by quotes and clichés.

See if you can relate to this scenario as an example of an intended feel good quote that just annoys the hell out of you: You approach a confidante seeking objective advice or practical help with a personal problem. You express yourself, warts and all and then ask for advice.

The person quickly tells you to 'hang in there', ' it will get better' or ' you will grow through what you go through'. Then there are the classic ones: 'keep your head up', 'what doesn't kill you makes you stronger', 'it'll all work out' and 'i'm praying for you'.

You really need practical help or solution based advice. You actually get platitudes.
The platitude professionalism that we get from time to time does have some value because a kind word will boost the spirit of someone who needs to be uplifted at that time. Sometimes we need more than words.

The irony that the words in this book have a feel good factor is not lost. The aim is to inspire you to action. I trust that you will find value in the thoughts expressed through these words and move forward with the right collective team.

This life has a way of being results-orientated in the dispensation of its blessings and rewards. To reap what you sow is a natural expectation, therefore, you have to 'work, work, work, work, work ' (to paraphrase Rihanna).

I really do encourage you to collaborate and work effectively with others. Just be discerning as to who you work with and upon whom you rely to manifest that which you envision. Be clear about what they are bringing to the table and how / why / where / when it fits into your vision. More is achieved by working with qualified people. All persons benefit and continue to develop in personal and professional capacities through such interactions.

Phenomenally successful musical groups and individuals prove the value of effective teamwork. Dispel the lie that you can do it alone. Create a powerful support system and make global power moves together.
Enough said.

4. STICKABILITY

You're wondering what stickability means, right?

Allow me to lay the foundation for explaining what it means by giving you its triple-tiered context. Firstly, I first heard the word used by someone I truly adore, reverently admire, genuinely appreciate and love unconditionally in this life and the next. Secondly, it is a coined term composed of two words: Stick and Ability. Thirdly, it is the essence of what Denzel Washington alluded to in this extract from his 2017-acceptance speech at the NAACP Image Awards for, among other qualities, his powerful performance in 'Fences'.

Washington also directed this adaptation of the August Wilson classic in which he had previously performed theatrically. Here's what he had to say:
"Without commitment you'll never start but more importantly without consistency you'll never finish...Ease is a greater threat to progress than hardship. So, keep moving. Keep growing. Keep learning..."

Let's break this down a little deeper to unearth the gems of wisdom in these few words:

"Without commitment you'll never start"

You must be dedicated and faithful to a particular cause or activity in the first place. Identifying what you are adhering to is paramount.

The level of attentiveness you give a cause or activity is an indication of how committed you are about making progress. Going the proverbial extra mile is standard behaviour when you are serious about doing what you agreed, within yourself, to do.

"Without consistency you'll never finish..."

Motivation will get you started but it's not enough. You must stay with it, see it through and be patient with the process.

You must have stickability. There is an unwavering focus required in order to keep doing something over and over again to manifest the vision.

It takes great sacrifice and effective work to complete what you started. This is why an athlete trains over and over and over again so the competition moments appear less daunting, e.g. when Mo Farah fell then got up automatically and kept going as discussed in Chapter 1: Cultivating your vision.

"Ease is a greater threat to progress than hardship".

Taking things at a leisurely pace may lead to personal complacency. Challenges bring out the best in you because you'll see how resilient you are. It's one thing to believe in your abilities. It's another thing when you are tested on what you thought you believed about yourself. Facing difficulties comes with blessings – once you go through them.

"So, keep moving. Keep growing. Keep learning".

Stay in the process of mastering your craft. Let continued professional development be at the forefront of your thinking. Appreciate the magnitude of your gifts coupled with your infinite potential to evolve.

Stickability, or a lack thereof, is one of the reasons many people lead unfulfilled lives. If you start something and do not finish it, then it's simply not done.

There may be valid excuses but that is just what they are – excuses. They are reasons we use to justify to ourselves (and others) as to why we have not completed specific tasks.

These kinds of excuses sound good, they are understandable, they make us feel better and they may even make sense. But guess what?
You still didn't finish what you started.

Excuses do not change the reality that your mission was not completed.
You may well have tried but to try is not the same as to do. In the latter part of the previous chapter 'Achieve more together', we looked at the confidante who gives well-intended platitudes when what you actually need is practical help.

Here's a scenario to support my thoughts on the non-productive nature of making excuses:
"I failed the exam but I tried my best". Evidently my trying was not good enough. The examiner was not impressed with my trying because it fell short of the expected criteria.

Trying did not give me the required grade any more than participating in the exam would automatically make me pass.

Trying and participating is not the same as action and results. Do you see where I'm coming from?

The word 'participating' has just triggered another thought I'd like to share with you. Life doesn't reward you for simply being alive. You have to be taking part in it. You need to engage with your life or as the British cockneys would say: "Get stuck in mate!".

Life rewards us with measurable results when we actively engage in creating our blessings. Being here on earth without progressing means we merely exist. Push forward within the realities of your current situation.
You are only competing with yourself to be better.

You are not in competition with anyone else and it is a pointless distraction to believe you are. Stay with your visions. Modify them on your terms. Handle your business. Foster the ability to stick with what you want for your life.

This is why it takes self-discipline to exercise your ability to stick with what you started. Learn how to see things through.

Stay close to and on top of the vision you are committed to bringing forth. Handle your business with laser sharp focus and avoid distractions. Invest in yourself.

Here's the ABC of how you develop or maintain Stickability:

A. Love your mission / project / activity and remember why you are doing it. The reason will keep you inspired and recharge you when it gets difficult.

B. Envision how you will feel when the mission / project / activity is complete and anchor that feeling in your subconscious mind right now.

See the finished product in your mind and it will help you to understand how every step you take in the present is necessary for the future achievement.

C. Put in the effective work, form alliances with the right people, reward yourself, be flexible yet focused in your approach, nurture your body, mind & soul and enjoy the process.

Stickability requires creative intelligence. It also means not allowing strength to become weakness. In this context we are understanding strength as the determination to stay with something no matter what.

This can also become a weakness if you fail to measure the progress you make by stubbornly staying with your agenda.

You may be engaged in a project because your detractors said you couldn't do it and you want to prove them wrong or let them eat their words.

There is a time and place for proving yourself.

The key is not to let others dictate when and how you prove yourself. This strength can be used against you as you end up moving to their agenda instead of your own.

They say you can't, you need to prove them wrong thus giving away your personal power in the process. There is no shame in knowing when to cease and desist in relation to unproductive missions, projects or activities. That's what I mean by not allowing strength to become weakness.

Let's wrap this up so we can explore the science of critical thinking in more detail in Chapter 5.

There is much value in finishing what we start and seeing things through.

It takes a special kind of person – a person like you – to exercise due diligence and patience when making things happen. History plays a symphony of strong stories about people who were committed to a higher cause.

Jamaica gives us Nanny of the Maroons who focused on strategically liberating her people from British rule and carving out independent territory. Winston Churchill played a sterling role as British Premier during the Blitz, Battle of Britain and Dunkirk.

Ethiopia had been one of the few states to withstand the scramble for Africa by major European powers in the late 19th century due to the leadership of Emperor Haile Selassie.

The point is not whether we hold their causes noble or even whether we agree with what they stood for. The point is that they were committed and commitment is an attribute of Stickability.

When you want to achieve something you must develop your ability to intelligently stick with it and measure your progress. You must put in the strategic work to keep mastering your craft and cultivate what you envision.

5. THE SCIENCE OF CRITICAL THINKING

"I love the way Candace Owens thinks"

were seven words tweeted on April 21, 2018 by Kanye West that triggered passionate responses on social media platforms. You may research these individuals at your leisure and agree or disagree with their positions on issues. If you are familiar with Candace or Kanye you will know that they are polarizing figures simply for how they think and confidently express themselves.

The core of this chapter is about developing your power to exercise independent thought. This chapter is focused on the analysis of facts to form a judgement. Diversity, inclusion and political correctness are terms that are currently in vogue. It's as if anything goes as long as these three entities are involved in some way. Things get very sensitive when you express views that seem to go against the perceived tide of pro-diversity, inclusion and political correctness. A person holding opposing views to the general narrative does not make them the devil incarnate, wrong or stupid. Their views are simply different to yours.

You may not agree with my reasoning, spiritual belief system, politics, eating habits or lifestyle.

Does that mean you should remain mute to avoid offending me? There are existing laws governing hate speech. I am talking about the unwillingness to respect or allow other perspectives on given issues.

What we are exploring here is the unreasonable pressure put on people who analyse things differently from the common narrative. The weight placed on persons who come to logical conclusions based on presented facts. We are talking about the inner strength required to guide your brain against falling for the everyday nonsense that dumbs your intellect. There is a science to training your mind to function from fact, logic and reason rather than emotion, hearsay and conjecture.

Religious philosophy is a rather strange animal. Strange in that every organised religion claims its monopoly on 'the truth', which implies that everyone else is wrong. Promotion of 'the truth' is vital to recruit others and share this version of liberating truth.

This liberating truth normally impacts all aspects of the lives of those who believe in it. All major achievements are accredited to the belief system.

Time, money, blood, sweat and tears are put into the preservation of this truth because it is perceived as the only way forward in this life. Organised religions pay lip service to the oneness of a supreme being and routinely convene joint meetings in their attempts to establish common ground.

Far be it for me to question the noble motives of such outreach. This much is for certain: all participants in these outreach efforts return to their specific ways of living their liberating truth however enlighteningly polite the interfaith discourse.

I have mentioned organised religion so I may as well mention another sensitive subject: race.
Race is a similarly contentious construct in that the notion of Caucasian supremacy has systematically impacted people with higher doses of melanin to believe that they are inferior. Ironically, a hierarchical system has developed amongst people with more melanin ranging from the lighter to the darker with the darker at the bottom of this spectrum.
The actual and perceived benefits of being Caucasian have impacted the minds, lifestyles and wherewithal of people with higher doses of melanin in all avenues of human endeavour.

Gender is still an embattled arena as we seek to establish and come to terms with what it means to be male, female, transgender, non-binary gender and any other understanding of the human experience. Persons who use a wheelchair, or considered less able in some way, often struggle to be respected as people for the dynamic contributions they make in society. They are differently abled – as we all are to some extent or another.

Culture, lifestyle, sexual preference and dissenting opinions all have a role in defining what it means to be human. Please analyse, rather than emotionally react to, the views expressed so far in this chapter because this too is an exercise in critical thinking.

My purpose of painting this tapestry of sensitive (or some may argue politically incorrect) observations is that we are pulled in many mental directions. These directions are not figments of our imagination. They are real. What you believe, how you see race, how you choose to live your life, the way you define yourself and how you decide to deal with what life throws at you are not worked out through comforting words alone.

The examples in the above paragraphs may have been uncomfortable to read, yet I'm sure you could relate to at least one of the thoughts expressed. You thought about it even though it may have made you a little uneasy. You understood even though you may disagree with my perspective. This chapter is entitled: The Science of Critical Thinking.

It is a true blessing to be able to engage your mind in objective thought because many people simply do not analyse what they hear, see and believe. The science of critical thinking and the willingness to question what one reads or hears has nothing to do with intellectual / emotional acceptance of historical / mythical narratives.

You don't have to be religious to be a caring person or adhere to a particular doctrine to experience a better quality of life. No one school of thought or way of life has a monopoly on liberating truth. Everything is relative. If it works for you then count your blessings and stay in your liberated lane.

Be true to your core philosophy, lifestyle, culture etc. This universe respects diversity, nature understands mutuality and creation values inclusion. This is a reminder to be proud of who you are.

This is a timely clarion call to honour your ancestors, love your country and create a personal mission statement to remind yourself to value your likeness in the grand scheme of this experience called Life. This is a word of encouragement to be unapologetically you.

At this stage it's likely that your mind is racing. I'll also be bold enough to suggest that at least one of the following 6 thoughts / emotions entered your mind since reading this chapter:

1. You hadn't necessarily seen it that way before.

2. You hear what's been said but you are struggling to take on this fresh perspective.

3. You understand but it challenges your core beliefs so much that you feel you must reject this kind of thinking or at least ridicule it.

4. How dare Malik (use another term if you're vexed) write any of this!

5. A combination of all of the above plus your own (unprintable) internal feelings because I touched a nerve in your comfortable thought patterns.

6. I get it. I can work with it. Felt this way about this stuff for some time myself.

You know how you are feeling in this moment and only you know whether any combination or derivation of the above thoughts resonate with you.

One thing is for certain; you felt something about what you read. You created a moment to allow yourself to think on what you were reading. Other words for think are: ruminate, ponder, reflect or study. Other ways to understand thinking are to meditate upon, consider or contemplate.

You can reflect on anything in the same way that you can think what you want. What you think is not the issue here; it is how you think. We are discussing how you arrive at conclusions, the process you use to come up with certain views and the manner in which you decide the core values that shape your life.

The 'critical' part of critical thinking involves analysis of the merits of a particular thought, perspective or view. The science of critical thinking is about the way you analyse the consequences of particular actions or beliefs. It is about reasoned judgements that follow logic.

Critical thinking means you question certain conclusions and dissect given arguments instead of blindly accepting what you have been socially fed. It also involves objective analysis and evaluation before reaching an informed conclusion.

The willingness to engage in independent reflective thinking will support your ability to define what you believe and what to do. Critical thinking skills include observation, analysis, problem solving and clear communication.

The next step is an exercise in the art of thinking. Do you have the courage to question yourself about why you feel the way you do about certain things? Have you ever thought about why you believe what you believe? Were you raised to accept certain views as true because that's how it's always been? Do you have too much riding on the way you currently think? Do you have too much to lose to change now? When you think critically you begin to ask questions. Questions require answers. Answers initiate action. Action manifests change and change, dear reader, is an indication of growth.

Please rise above any distracting emotions by allowing your powerful mind to evolve into a dimension of higher thinking as you examine these four observations:
1. People move from friendly conversation to verbal abuse over the concept of god.
2. Wars were fought and are still fought over religion.

3. Alternative lifestyles have been mocked and vilified.
4. Race has been used to determine intelligence and social standing.

The evident folly in these observations suggests they should not make sense. That's if you are thinking critically. In reality you and I both know they happen and, sadly, make a lot of sense to some people.
We are nurtured to internalise ideas that are illogical when examined in the cold light of day.

Some of these ideas are intergenerational to the point where we do not even know why they are held. We just grow up knowing that this is how it is and so we pass it on.

Breaking this cycle of familiarity is hard. It is painful to question what we have been taught all our lives.

This is part of the reason many of us just go along to get along rather than rock the boat of accepted thought.

It's as though we blindly train our minds to unquestionably accept certain views.

Great advances in medicine, aviation, academia, science and technology only happened because a few brave people decided to question that which was considered normal.

History is replete with countries having used the science of critical thinking that resulted in measurable progress over time. Who would have imagined a world dominant Japan after the atomic bombings of Hiroshima and Nagasaki?

How has India become a technological powerhouse given the ravages of the 1948 partition? Why does Jamaica disproportionately dominate world athletics in addition to having given the world a spiritual way of life (Rastafarianism) a form of music (Reggae) and pioneered modern day veganism /plant-based eating since 1930 (Ital cooking)?

Be willing to evaluate an issue before forming an opinion. It comes out of a certain confidence in self or via specific collective validation.

It's the 'I am enough' or 'we are enough' feeling that requires no external validation. It is living authentically and in accordance with your core values.

My context for defining the art of critical thinking is that one ought to be able to look at an issue from different perspectives, hold a meditation, evaluate and then come to an informed conclusion. A critical thinker is someone who engages with opposing views without being rattled by the expression of said views.

Critical thinkers can analyse the message without attacking the messenger as seen in the powerful Kanye / Candace case study at the start of this chapter.

I'm simply encouraging you to engage in critical thinking by rising above emotively inherited views into a higher frequency of reasoning.

Cultivate the courage to question concepts that will impact your life. Develop the strength to trust your gut and how you feel about particular issues.

Logically formulate, clearly communicate and respect your own views on things. Form intelligent perspectives based on objective analysis and evaluation.

6. NOTHING BEATS COMMON SENSE

Many of us have been socialised to think that formal education trumps street knowledge or informal training.

We laud persons with undergraduate and postgraduate degrees or those with professional qualifications in their chosen areas of expertise. The years of study it takes to get any formal accreditation requires stickability and deserves respect.

On one hand you could say that formal education is necessary and a way to improve your standing in life.

On the other hand you may argue that unfocused formal education is pointless because you are lumbered with debt, have poor employment prospects and no work experience to compete for certain jobs.

There is a subtle snobbery from learned and lettered people against unlearned or unlettered people.

This, to some extent, is human nature. Your tribe closes ranks around itself as people gravitate towards those with whom they have certain things in common (we explore tribal connections in Chapter 12: About Diversity).

Let's discuss two basic examples of how people are attracted to people with whom they have something in common.

1. *Smokers. A smoker needing a lighter will look around for someone smoking and approach them with laser beam focus to ask the all-important question: 'Do you have a light?' Someone who vapes will automatically strike up a conversation with a fellow vaper during a conference break.*

2. *Networkers. People attending a networking event generally gravitate towards people they know, vaguely know or those they recognise from their social media friends lists. It is understandable that we socialise among the people with whom we have things in common. Your socialisation should not be limited to these criteria.*

The impact of globalisation means that peoples of diverse cultures interact at a faster and more meaningful pace. People tend to carry aspects of their culture with them wherever they go.

Mixing with people outside your tribe or frame of reference will broaden your understanding of today's world thus raising your level of global awareness.

It's also better for business and the building of interpersonal relationships.

If I need major surgery, it is comforting to know that the surgeon is formally qualified and experienced before that scalpel touches my flesh. The individual handling my complex legal affairs should, at least, have a law degree to effectively represent my interests.

An architect had better be properly trained when drawing up the blueprint for my ideal home.

Interest in medicine by watching a few medical based television shows will not comfort me.

A passion for justice or a love of buildings will not influence me to engage with you professionally.

Formal education is vital as it allows you to legally practice and sustain a career in your chosen field. It validates you as an expert. It proves you are a specialist who can be taken seriously in your field. It is right and prudent that certain professions require proper certification in order to practice professionally.

There are other professions / careers / jobs where experience qualifies the individual and industry specific test standards are sufficient.

In these careers, formal qualifications are not necessarily a requirement and the level of professionalism / work ethic / knowledge of craft are of the highest calibre. There are people who simply did not have the opportunity, means or desire to access higher learning yet lead fruitful lives in their chosen careers.

A disciplined self-taught designer delivers fabulous creations, as does a naturally talented artist or skilled carpenter. Someone cultivated in the healing ways of their ancestors by using natural herbs and particular foods to reduce ailments and maintain good health should not be ignored.

You can think of other examples, as I'm sure you get the gist of my reasoning.

Check the stories of business people from humble beginnings anywhere in the world. You will find quite a few of them are successful because they acted on gut instinct and passion for what they do. They also employed people to do all the other things that needed to be done.

Their evident lack of major formal academic qualifications may be seen as an asset based on the clear evidence of what they have produced plus the extent of their success. They also appear to engage in critical thinking.

Learning and the quest for knowledge ought to be a lifelong pursuit. It is always useful to invest in your personal development. Reading this book is evidence that you already understand that life is about improving yourself in as many ways as possible.

You are powerful in your brilliance whether you are blessed with high academic learning or blessed without high academic learning. It is how you use what you have that is ultimately important.

Comparing yourself with someone else is a stupid exercise plus a waste of valuable time. There will only ever be one authentic version of you. Focus on that.

We are programmed to validate ourselves through likes on a social media post, the signing of an online petition, the angle of a selfie or by reposting a misleading and out-dated article (as if we are roving reporters with the exclusive on another alternative fact or fake news update).

The comfort of blindly following others has usurped the power of personal leadership.

Value the worth in your life experience to date. Commit to additional learning in order to improve your quality of life. Engage in activities that expand your mind no matter what your academic achievements are at this point.

My argument is that academic achievements make us specialists in specific areas – not all areas.

There is no need to be haughty about academic expertise because the more we know is the more there is to know.

Omniscience is beyond the realm of mere mortals. Never feel inferior about your lack of academic qualifications because there are things you know very well and there is still so much more to learn. There is no need to feel confused or deflated by missed opportunities in academia because you are clearly intelligent and we are all engaged in this life cycle of fulfilling our potential.

Society will surely define you if you fail to define yourself. Appreciate and celebrate what you've done thus far. Now take a moment to congratulate yourself!

These expressed thoughts are not limited to weighing the merits of academic achievement per se. They are using academics as an example of how we often measure our self-worth according to standards that are imposed on us.

Being functionally illiterate is dangerous in any culture. As you proceed to further your learning please make sure that you study strategically with a genuine love for what you are absorbing into your mind. All you've studied so far has already been achieved.

What is your legacy? What contribution are you making to the world? Exercise some stickability to what you may be studying now. Give serious thought about the learning you engage with for your future.

Trust your gut instinct / conscience / self-accusing spirit / inner voice to guide you aright. Continue to cultivate your intelligence in a world that often rewards ignorance and promotes mediocrity.

What you do (job) and what you know (academic learning) is not the essence of who you are. It is foolhardy to only see the worth within you through this prism of job description and higher learning.

A rich famous celebrity is a rich famous celebrity yet such a person is tagged as a 'role model' sooner or later. The same applies to musicians, reality show stars and the like.

Though some deserve such an accolade, it's the automatic presumption of role model status that is problematic. What about your parent, guardian, relative, mentor, best friend, favourite teacher, godparent, grandparent et al. who you see regularly and who sacrifice endlessly?

They are the bona fide role models. They have directly earned that title in your life. They lead by example and positively impact your life because they have helped cultivate your core values.

It's as if the pendulum of being a role model has swung away from those who prove they are and more towards those who satisfy the desire for sport and play in our lives.

This presumption of role model status is understandable. It is also somewhat troubling.

The famous are held to a higher standard than the not-so-famous and any personal mistake or error in judgement is treated and publicised as the modern day version of one of the seven deadly sins.

Being rich and famous can mean more money and more problems. It can also mean the freedom to decide how you live and what you purchase.

Advertising creates the desire to purchase a product, service or experience. This call to action goes deep in our subconscious.

It harbours like a boat at rest until we see the object of our desire once again e.g. seeing an advert for a popular beverage, automatically feeling thirsty then going to the store to purchase said liquid dose of refined sugar and other chemicals.

Media masters the manipulative machinations behind those we manage to inherently idolise. We subliminally accept the mundane nature of our lives and live vicariously through the perceived excitement of reality television, music videos and other entertainment distractions. We compare our ordinary lives with their seemingly fabulous ones and find ourselves coming up short every single time.

The weight of interpersonal comparison is a heavy burden yet many of us bear the burden because we live in a world that subliminally promotes it.

Being inspired by the work and achievements of another human being is empowering.

It's sensible to emulate their success strategies. It is equally important to value the good within yourself.

Continue to invest in your personal development. Invest in ways that bolster your skillset.

Appreciating your unique skills and putting them to work will prove both redemptive and financially rewarding in the long run.

"You are driven by your own heart, by your talent and you are driven by your instinct and if you start to look at what people are doing to the left of you or to the right of you: you are going to lose that clarity of thought. Own your decisions and own who you are but without apology".

-Anna Wintour

7. WHEN MEMES AREN'T ENOUGH

At the end of the Clifton Suspension Bridge in Bristol, UK there is a sign that reads 'Talk to us. Call Samaritans for free 116 123'. Chad Varah founded Samaritans in 1953, as he believed there should be a helpline for people to call if they were feeling suicidal. People choose to leave this life experience for a myriad of reasons, some too complex to comprehend. Each decision to commit suicide comes with a backstory that belonged to someone who had visions, desired love and experienced many of the common realities that you and I face. They were human beings who simply had enough and considered it best to permanently escape from their pain.

Living life without purpose carries its own burden. Appearances can be deceptive. 'I'm fine' doesn't necessarily mean everything's ok. Few people really and truly care about how you are. They ask just to appear pleasant. It could even be argued that most people genuinely don't give a
......

The emotional cost of living is as real as the financial cost of living. Both require attention in line with the core values that you deem important. Having a goal, vision or idea is cool. You also need to create time to pursue that goal, vision or idea.

Some days can be more difficult than others. You may just feel unmotivated, tired or desire a break from your daily routine. Circumstances may have derailed your carefully thought out plans. Family commitments will make you forget who you are due to the demands they regularly make on your life.

Over time you appear to be a function like mother, employee, husband, provider, chef, partner, confidante, reliable friend as opposed to a human being with ambitions, visions and ideas. Over time you become known for what you do rather than who you are. Establishing who you are involves being positively selfish.

This includes creating a space for yourself in the midst of these competing demands. It takes courage to eventually say 'no', 'stop', 'I'm not available'. You need to do something for yourself without feeling guilty about not being there for someone else.

You simply need to prioritise yourself in the same way that you prioritised others. This is an act of Self Love (which reminds me of the Jaguar Wright song of the same title and the unique spin she takes on the subject.)

A smiling face can mask pain that may never be spoken of and a charming disposition may hide invisible scars that never heal. Jazz musicians of a certain era were known for either dabbling in or being hooked on certain illegal drugs.

Can you imagine the heart wrenching dehumanization of selling out a venue yet not being allowed to sit in the same audience afterwards? How about selling thousands of records but suffering the indignity of not having your face on the (then) vinyl album cover? Couple that with the social climate that rendered you subhuman despite your obvious brilliance and one may begin to appreciate why a temporary relief through drugs was sought.

Pain always seeks a remedy. Illegal and legal drugs such as cigarettes and alcohol temporarily ease pain. People who commit suicide aim to permanently ease their pain and people on the brink of suicide also seek this release from their pain.

A little compassion, or even empathy, is all that's being suggested around this subject. Only you really know how low you feel at times. Depression and all manifestations of mental ill health should be approached with a degree of compassion. Do you have your act fully together? Does anyone? Indulge me for a few more minutes whilst I clarify my argument around pain and drugs.

I understand the need to escape the rigour of personal pain. Using legal and illegal drugs may numb temporarily. It's understandable but short-lived. It supresses the problem but never solves it. I recommend that we discuss it, have open minded conversations and implement healthy measures to effectively cope with the personal pain.

My intention is to positively influence you to become more reflective and less judgemental. More understanding, less haughty. More kind, less maliciously dismissive. More objective, less subjective. More informed and less emotive in your conclusions. Are you with me?

Let's explore some coping mechanisms and practical tools because inspirational memes and kind words aren't enough when you want to make measurable progress.

Receiving the positivity from the utterance of a kind word has the power to uplift your soul. A simple telephone call can mean so much. A WhatsApp voice-note can change someone's life. So can a brief inspirational message or heartfelt hug.

There are also situations so dire that such deeds have no impact on your state of mind. Sometimes there's no positive word, uplifting message or comforting hug. There may be times when you have little or no support.

Whatever the circumstances you still have to dig deep within to find ways to cope or find ways just to get through the day. Please remember that you still have yourself especially in times when a kind word, message or hug is not available.

*Keep yourself focused on surviving each day until you are strong enough to walk in your power on a daily basis. Stand firm in the knowledge that **"bad vibes don't last, they always pass"** as Ini Kamoze reflectively expressed in his song 'Them Thing Deh'. Remember a good time in your life and feed on that memory during rough moments.*

It takes resilience, unconditional support and self-belief to withstand the difficult times that you will go through. That we go through. That empowered people go through.

Sometimes you're in such a bad place that you don't want to hear any damn uplifting words or clichéd platitudes about how things will get better. People can always pray for you but, in hard times, you need some practical support or real coping mechanisms.
We shall now focus on three real exercises that will help you get through the rough times.

1. ***CREATE A DAILY ROUTINE.*** *Have one thing you do each day without fail. One thing you do without making excuses. One thing you prioritise no matter what. The idea of a routine is that you create a regular moment to focus yourself by doing something consistently.*

It creates a perfect space where all that really matters is you and your activity.

This gives you the freedom to experience inner peace for that moment which will, in turn, boost your spirit and help you to face all difficulties on given issues (the way you electrically charge your cellular phone when the battery is going flat.)

Routines also bring a sense of order when other aspects of your life are out of kilter. Routine promotes self-discipline.

2. ***DO IT FOR LOVE****. Think of at least one person who wants the best for you. Allow yourself to feel how disappointed that person would be if you just gave up on life without fighting. Now convert the imagined disappointment into fuel for positive action. Let your love for this person inspire you to get through the day. Apply this imagined situation even if the person has transcended this life because flesh fails but spirit lives forever.*

Honour the memory of that person by being productive.

You may even speak with him / her quietly in your mind to seek guidance based on previous conversations you both had.

Keep a loved one's picture near you as a physical reminder of your true inspiration.

3. **IS THIS HOW MY STORY ENDS?** *Ask yourself this simple question then answer it honestly. As the captain of your life's ship you have a major influence on the route of your life's journey. You must face any situation that is trying to derail your progress. 'Tis a mere obstacle to surpass in the unfolding of your life. You have been through too much, invested much time and sacrificed immensely.*

Close your eyes and picture the ending you want. Picture your life that is forming through the pieces of this vision- orientated jigsaw puzzle. Do you see how magnificent it is? That's the ending you want. That is how this story ends. That's why you face and overcome all obstacles. This is your story, so you must create the ending you want.

This chapter is also about how you protect yourself against the darker aspects of your tortured self. It's about how you cope when no one is looking.

This chapter is a healing balm in the Gilead of your lonesome nights as the voices circle your mind with thoughts that no one hears but you.
A slow drip of water in an enamel bath will leave an impenetrable stain over time.

So, it is with the challenges of life as they drip on your soul. They leave emotional scarring that is not always clear to the naked eye. You can smile yet be pained. You can easily say 'I'm fine' when things are far from okay with you.

You may seem filled with the joy of life yet unsure if you even want to see tomorrow. You may be riddled with remorse for past mess-ups and unable to rise from the mental sewer of personal disappointment and internal rage. Church folks have a song that partly says, "Nobody knows the trouble I've seen. Nobody knows but Jesus".

There is some stuff you've been through (or are going through) that only a higher power can possibly know about. After a while it doesn't take much to send you over the edge in one way or another. It is at this point that one is most vulnerable and numbing the pain, temporarily or permanently, is all that matters.
It is hard to move from this dark place to a brighter reality.
It is hard, but not impossible.

This is the real beauty of self-empowerment strategies because they guide you to a better state of being and consistently drive you to cultivate your visions.

Mental ill health is real. I refuse to accept that the only persons suffering mental ill health are those legally sectioned or formally diagnosed.

This personal conclusion is based on the global and historical observation of 'man's inhumanity to man'. The evil wrought by human hands comes from a certain mindset that is clearly demented.

Social media platforms, podcasts, Internet based programming and other forms of entertainment are designed to flood our minds with specific streams of thought.

Freedom of expression is cool. So is the need to be discerning about what you allow to penetrate your mind.

Be selective about what you watch and listen to. Constant exposure to negativity takes its toll on how you think.

Positive exposure to experiences and thoughts that edify your spirit will help to maintain a healthy level of harmony in your life. This is why it is useful to have rituals that uplift your mind, body and soul. Here are 3 such productive rituals to consider:

GIVE THANKS FOR LIFE AND ALL YOUR BLESSINGS. *Do this on a daily basis because it serves as a reminder that some aspects of your life are going well. There is always one thing to be thankful for. In moments when everything feels wrong, remember one thing that's going right.*

That one thing may lead to the remembrance of another and another thus creating a domino effect of gratitude. The mind is powerful when programmed correctly. It is equally self-defeating or even dangerous when infused with unproductive thought patterns.

SEE THE SITUATION THROUGH THE EYES OF YOUR INNER CHILD. *I'm suggesting that you look at the situation with simplicity. Ignore the tendency to complicate the issue and just view it for what it is. One of the qualities that adults lose over time is the ability to simplify perspectives.*

With time we grow and mature, however, the songs of innocence and experience that William Blake spoke of should still beam brightly in our hearts and minds. Aim to see a particular issue for how it is rather than what you'd like it to be. It saves time, unnecessary headache and allows a solution to present itself.

ENGAGE MIND. TRAIN BODY. NOURISH SOUL.
Look after yourself by putting life-giving foods into your body. Water hydrates so drink it regularly to reap some of the other amazing benefits. Find joy in experiences rather than just via things.

Read views you oppose because they strengthen your ability to articulate and have a deeper understanding of your perspective. Schedule some physical exercise into your week. Listen to your favourite song or piece of music. Bake a delicious cake. Try scuba diving or travel to a part of your country you've never been before.

Go to Jamaica.
Do something to help you make it through the fire of your current challenge.
Commit to make it through and you will.
We will.

*Be patient with your progress and remember that there are no shortcuts to success. You will get there eventually (wherever **there** is).*
*This is our opportunity to live productive manifestations of our lives. Be present – even though many of us are tempted to impatiently ask ourselves: **Are we there yet?***

Are we there yet?
Where is this 'there' that we seek?
This elusive and seemingly elusive destination that we should all supposedly want to reach.
What is so great about 'there' that requires us to be dissatisfied with 'here'?
Having dreams is okay, 'To dream the impossible dream'
To have hope is a must
Aspirations and inspirations are a necessary food group but not at the expense of the here and now
Right here. Right now.
Right here. Right now.

Living in the moment, however fleeting
Embracing the grace given for today. Seize the day!
Squeeze out of it all that you can
(For) tomorrow is not promised so make use of today while you can.

Why the rush to see what else is on offer?
In our haste for the next, we may deny the now
Our moreish disposition rewarded with chronic indigestion
Blinded by the vision of what 'there' will be like
Enticed by the stories of those who've 'arrived'
In an age of fake news, we'd do well to be wise.

Forever wanting, never satisfied
Maybe that gaping hole is of our own making
because it can be filled anywhere but 'there'.

Let's try living in the now
Right here. Right now. Right here. Right now.
This is your life, this is my life,
It may not all be pretty,
All things may not be aligned and it's happening
live
But we're here, we're now.
So why ask 'are we there yet? When we are
already here,
Which, who knows, could actually be our 'there'

-Janice M Whyne

8. FRIENDS & RELATIONSHIPS

Genuine friendships and beneficial relationships are priceless. They are also empowering, hence, the subject of this chapter. The adjectives 'genuine' and 'beneficial' are included to clarify and contextualize this contemplation. The contextual clarification is necessary because social media uses the term 'friends' and people even refer to casual acquaintances as 'friends'.

I think a friend is loyal, trustworthy and loves unconditionally. Friendship comes with a ride or die dynamic and its bona fide to the core. Friendship transcends time, space and circumstance. You don't always agree but you always have each other's back.

The running order for this chapter is that we shall commence with thoughts on friends, proceed to relationships and close out by summarizing the overall perspective.

Friends. 'Good fren beta than pocket money' is a Jamaican saying that reminds us that good friends are more precious than even the money in our pockets. They are invaluable. Money is necessary and impacts our standard of living.

Good friends will validate and love us in ways that money cannot. One entity is tangible (money) whilst the other (friendship) is an experience that includes feelings, connecting and bonding.

Friendship is rooted in a love that embraces difference, personal growth and any other issues.

Loyalty is a mutually shared value and there is a sense of protecting each other that does not have to be verbally expressed.

Confidentiality is another feature of this dynamic. Real love, in this context, has a way of making you feel everything's going to be okay with this friend by your side.
When you seek their advice; you know they'll come from an objective place and always have your best interest at heart.

They hold you up when you feel down while making sure you act to change your current situation for the better.

Longevity is cool but it's more about the quality of the friendship rather than the length of time you have known each other.

Some people enter our lives for a fixed period to do their work and then leave. This in no way diminishes their contribution in our lives. It is a very special experience to have the blessing of long-term friendships (as previously discussed in Chapter 3: Achieve More Together).

Same sex friendships bring natural empathy to the equation. They are an integral part in your personal development. Being gender specific, I recall the writing of T.D. Jakes in his brilliant book **He-motions** *where he explains that every man needs a man in his life.*

I agree with this perspective, as there are times when the 'sledgehammer to a mustard seed' approach is needed to correct particular behaviours through a man-to-man conversation. The same may be logically inferred in the case of women and with regard to how one gender identifies.

The biased proposition is that the more you have in common with someone, the more likely it is for you to identify with and relate to them. Ensuing conversations may be more straightforward with less regard to political correctness or overly sensitive sensibilities.

Intergender friendships offer a glimpse into the mind of the other. A natural balance follows through as night is to day or sun is to moon. A similar chemistry develops with those who identify by the gender of their choice.

There is compatibility through the common understanding of a shared experience.

"A true friend knows your weaknesses but shows you your strengths; feels your fears but fortifies your faith; sees your anxieties but frees your spirit; recognises your disabilities but emphasises your possibilities"
—William Arthur Ward

Relationships. We need to interact with others in this experience called life. We connect as social beings via the old boys / girls network, blatant nepotism, a friend of a friend, preference due to patriotism or any of the other human dynamics.

Life has taught and is still teaching me the importance of cherishing positive relationships. I was aware of this importance on an intellectual level yet my actions could often be interpreted as anything but aware.

Being aware of but acting contrary to said awareness is counterproductive. It also means that this awareness had not been understood on a subconscious / spiritual level hence the contrary action. When you truly know better, then it's useful to actually do better.

Relationships reasonably require reciprocity.

You give and the other person gives thus we give to each other resulting in a mutually beneficial exchange. Knowing, trusting and / or liking someone puts you in a stronger position to stay connected with them.

It impacts how you regard and behave towards each other and the same can be said for groups of people.

Handling people properly can be very subjective and contextual.

Subjective because its natural to bring your personal predilections to the fore when relating to people and contextual in the sense that certain circumstances can bring out the best and worst in you.

We establish rules of engagement as to how we conduct certain relationships.

These may evolve over time in personal domestic connections (e.g. a marriage), between a specific group of people (e.g. a team sport) or may even be agreed at the inception of said relationship (e.g. a business contract)

We observe certain protocols when we interact with people with whom we are familiar.

Certainty in the manner we relate is an empowering tool because the expectations are clear and there is a genuine appreciation as to how our actions contribute to the common good.

This is partly why countries have trading blocs, why diplomats and ambassadors spend so much time socialising, why work colleagues go for 'after work' drinks, why incarcerated cell mates remain civil and seldom snitch, why corporate entertainment closes a deal, why theologically opposed groups have interfaith prayer breakfasts, why enemies form alliances against a common foe and why your neighbours say 'good morning' then briefly smile.

The way you connect with someone can be a gift that keeps on giving or a poisoned chalice that is best discarded. You will not get along with everyone so it's absurd to bother trying.

You may be in (a). a work environment or even (b.) a personal situation where great effort is required in relating to someone you simply cannot stand being around.

Yet you chose to be around them due to (a.) getting your salary or (b.) the complications of family life. A compromise is necessary in either situation even though you'd sometimes prefer to just walk away.

This is the real nature of some relationships. The point of this chapter is to contemplate on ways to positively navigate these complex interpersonal issues. Life does not always go according to plan so you must learn to deal with difficult people and challenging circumstances. Human nature is such that interacting with people presents particular problems.

People are the basis of human relationships, so it simply makes sense to invest time in understanding how to sail the sea of uncertainty surrounding relationships.

The better the relationship, the stronger the bond. The strength of the bond empowers the parties to withstand the problems or misunderstandings that come up from time to time.

Investing in good friends and developing meaningful relationships are some of the essential ingredients for a successful life.

Do you remember that friend who came in your time of need?
The one who is a friend in deed?
The person who recommended your skill to someone else?
The people who vouch for you?

I asked you the above questions to further evidence the fact that empowerment comes from within yourself. The universe is within.

Discipline yourself to do all that is necessary to improve your life experience.

You are the only one who knows whether you answered the questions.

Answering them is good for you because it develops your ability to master yourself to do what's right for you especially when no one is looking at you, cheering you on or checking up on you. This is similar to the sacrifices you will make to stay on top of your game and in the mastery of your craft.

You will sacrifice in ways that no one may ever be aware of. It's not an easy road, many see the glamour and the glitter, so they think it's a bed of roses, but who feels it knows (paraphrasing Mark 'Buju Banton' Myrie).

The questions serve as a microcosm of the macrocosm that will guarantee your success in life. Business, personal, community and family growth is predicated on the strength of the interdependent relationships.
The quality of one's friends and relationships are why some people get what they envision while others don't.
I want you to always remember that there are experiences you still desire and things you are still committed to doing in your life. Reality shows, featuring a range of characters, are very popular right now. Do you ever wonder how history will speak of this televisual phenomenon?

If you are an ardent fan, you'll see that the people you admire are getting on with their lives. They are getting paid while you admire, read about and watch them.
Imagine that.

Will you write, direct and star in the progressive show of your life in real time? Think of the challenges your people have overcome thus far and you will learn that the blueprint is already there to help cultivate your visions.

One of the benefits of reading these contemplations is to access empowering tools that you can start using immediately.

Another benefit is hearing perspectives that will help you to build on what you already know.
It's all in the application of the knowledge e.g. you can imagine driving a nice car all day but it helps if you actually learn how to drive. Talking about doing something only matters once you've done it.

Quoting positive affirmations requires consistent action for them to truly materialise.

As you empower yourself to succeed you need to build with the right tools and know how to utilise effective strategies. The science of critical thinking is enhanced by mental emancipation.
This is the reason you are in deep thought and motivated by the views shared so far.

This is why you have read, continue to read and will most definitely re-read these ideas as you share and discuss these perspectives with others.

Here's something else to consider as we contemplate this subject of friends & relationships – they may go sour (as in hit rock bottom) with no possibility of being rekindled.

It is not always easy or even necessary to apportion blame when things go wrong.

The lessons learned should be considered and the healing needs to begin - for you.

Treasure the good memories.

Value the progress you made when the relationships were in a better state. You will bounce back eventually.

This is why in such situations you must stay in the process of healing and not make similar mistakes. The yin / yang of life brings duality and balance. Putting disappointments in the unemotional context they belong is imperative for personal development.

I know that having genuine friends and beneficial relationships are some of the most beautiful and comforting experiences in my life. So, do you because it takes a special kind of person to be a member of our empowerment tribe.

Let's continue to nurture our friends & relationships on this cool journey towards being the best version of us. This is us.

I encourage you to think of those people who hold a special place in your life and also utter a kind word to them now.

Think of the people who are at the centre of your world and send some positive energies to them in this moment.

Now caste your eye on the next page to connect with my simple homage to my Inner Circle.

Inner Circle,

One of my best-loved pianists with a beautiful soul simply says 'You know who you are' when referring to people who are close to her.

I connect with her sentiment in this moment.

You are cherished for a plethora of personal reasons. I will strive to be worthy of your love and be of value in your lives.
Individually and as a collective, you complete me.

I am because you are and you are because I am.

Our interdependence is natural.
We have an unconditional and sacred connection that transcends time, circumstance and space.

Give thanks, blessed love.

9. SUCCESS

Writers often talk about the importance of why they must write and how location inspires their content. Allow me to speak to the latter part of this sentence for a couple seconds.

Stay with me during this vivid recollection of the most serene view of the Caribbean Sea from the verandah at the home of a decent, Jehovah fearing lady in the thriving district of Cove, Hanover, Jamaica.

The view is simply picturesque.

The best way to attempt to describe this visual nirvana is by quoting a few lines from the song 'Speechless' by Natalie 'The Floacist' Stewart: **"No words can describe what my eyes caress and for the first time in my life – I'm speechless".**

Jamaica (Xaymaca) is an island that understands mutuality. Jamaica understands the benefits of pooling the skills and talents of all her people in the pursuit of collective visions. It is also a country that is worthy of dedicating one's life to. National advancement is predicated on the individual progress of all her citizens.

Patriotic politicians aim to put policies in place so that people patiently progress. Problems abound yet there is a cultural energy that makes the best out of every circumstance. There are lovely beaches, everyday expressions of our Taino & African heritage, a spectrum of creatively resilient people, technological advancement and positive vibrations in Jamaica.

The views are breathtakingly sublime.

Jamaica has a topography that must be experienced to be genuinely appreciated. The food, intellectual culture and daily happenings create a vibrant hub of humanity.

The world has many picturesque landscapes inhabited by people with great intellect and magnificent culture. This globe reflects the physical joy of creation in all its glory through diverse culture expressions, delicious food, varied belief systems, national achievements, academic prowess and different ways of life.

Travel expands the mind by creating frames of reference other than the ones with which we are familiar.

Success starts in your mind.

You can travel in your mind to places you've never been – to witness things you are yet to do – in ways that may seem unimaginable. You can physically go to other parts of your village, town, parish, country or continent to stimulate your thinking. In the absence of the opportunity to physically travel you can rearrange your living space to create fresh energy.

If that proves impractical then you can always resort to escaping in your mind by engaging your imagination. Changing your surroundings will always boost your energy level, make you feel better and bring a fresh perspective to living.

Breaking the cycle of one's daily routine is highly beneficial. Consistency is key to making things happen, at the same time, failure to review routines can hinder progress. You become more focused after creating moments to recharge, reassess and move ahead with clarity. It's about how we use what we have and the way we apply the resources at our disposal.

Seeing the value in where you are right now helps to guide your steps to where you are going in the future. Where are you going in the future can be linked with your imagination or what you visualise.

Success starts in your mind. This is why it is most beneficial to empower yourself to succeed. There are a range of techniques and a variety of books that associate success with being rich as though money and success are synonyms.

The issue with the connotation of success equalling money is that a lack of money means you're a failure. It implies that scraping to pay your bills and struggling to support your family means you are basically not doing well.

A rich male footballer is just that: Rich. Male. Footballer. He is successful if he sets out to do everything necessary to be his best self in his chosen field. He is successful because of what he did to get to where he is rather than being successful due to being rich.

Being rich and being successful are not synonymous states of being. If you aim to be rich (based on your understanding of how much 'rich' means) and you achieve this objective, then you should consider yourself successful in that regard.

COMMIT TO A VISION
DEVELOP A PLAN
MAKE IT HAPPEN

Success is personal. It is subjective. There are individual values that measure the standard and specific evidence to prove its attainment. Success is that moment when you have done what you set out to do.

Success is that special feeling and sense of achievement you experience when your mission has been accomplished. What defines success for me may not be the same for you, yet we both experience it when we achieve whatever we commit ourselves to do.

Respect the power already within yourself to define what your success looks like. Don't allow anyone to define what success should mean to you.

Success is personal. Your mind rankles under the pressure of comparing yourself to other people. You may hear comments like: 'Why can't you be normal?' ' Your sister never does that', 'Get your education so you can have a steady job', 'Our religion doesn't permit that', 'You should study this because there's good money in this industry', 'That is not part of our culture'.

I'm sure you get the gist of where we are going with these examples.

I'm only encouraging you to embrace and accept all that you already are. This is one of the hardest things to do in a world that promotes groupthink, fitting in with what's acceptable and the denigration of individuality.

The irony is that success comes by accepting and loving yourself just as you are. All other improvements are predicated on self-acceptance through the utilisation of empowering practises to cultivate what you want to achieve in this life.

"It's bad to have a job and not invest in yourself at the same time"

–Dame Dash

The contemplations in this chapter are simply to explain that success should always be defined by the standards you first set for yourself as you pursue what you envision. Acknowledge and check any negative internal conversations that you may have with yourself because they too will hold you back.

Defining and then deciding what success means to you is where the real power dwells. It's a slick trick of this world to make us believe that success is only achieved in particular ways, by certain people and according to narrowly prescribed standards. When we buy into these narrowly prescribed standards we do two things:

(1) Ignore and lose sight of who we truly are.

(2) Stifle all the ambition, growth and development we need to cultivate who we were born to be.

You'll remember from previous chapters that we look at practical scenarios to support or explain some of the written thoughts I seek to express. Here's another scenario with suggested solutions for you to think about.

Scenario:
The trajectory of your life takes a direction that is not in sync with your spirit thus creating an internal battle. You still have visions of what you are capable of, however, you battle with yourself to do anything about it.

This imbalance between your visions and your lack of results frustrates you every day. It makes you anxious and you experience intense mood swings.

This is all going on inside you yet when anyone asks how you are, you automatically reply 'I'm fine'.

This pretence is now your comfort mechanism. It is a heavy burden to wear the mask of happiness when your life seems filled with sadness. It gets even heavier when you begin to fear what you may look like if you took off the mask.

This mask has now become a tool to cope with your internal frustration and your private pain.

Solution:
1. *Speak with someone you trust who is capable of listening to you objectively.*

2. *Seek qualified / spiritual support to face the difficulty and create practical solutions.*

3. *Ask yourself if this is the life you want. Now decide to do something about it.*

4. *Think of one person or reason to keep going for another minute. Another hour. Another day. That person or reason will create a positive vibration inside you and*

make you smile awhile and give your pain a rest. The more you think about the person or reason, the longer you will shift your energy to an uplifting state of consciousness.

5. *Spend a little time alone so you can hear yourself think. Do something that makes you smile. It'll remind you that you deserve happiness in your life. Anchor that feeling and aim to get more of that feeling on a daily basis.*

One of the benefits of engaging in self-empowerment is that it gives you practical weapons to deploy in this war within you.

It provides tools that can be used when you lie alone in your bed / as you sit alone in your prison cell / as you stand alone in the crowd / when you drift off into your own thoughts at a family barbecue / when you idly do your household chores or when you try to block out an overly conversational passenger beside you on a long-haul flight.

Engaging in self-empowerment helps you get answers for the questions you feel in your heart. It gives you answers to the questions that are too painful to ask out loud.

To ask them out loud will somehow make them more real than they already are.

Success is how you see it and any self-doubt must be checked before it wrecks your progress. These thoughts on success go beyond the platitudes and the feel good factors. This strategy is aimed at increasing your productivity in real ways and in this lifetime.

Reading, praying, reasoning, emoting and even intellectualising about ways to deal with issues in your life are useful exercises because they help to provide much needed solutions. Whilst these exercises are useful, they are not enough.

My opinion is that whilst they may prove cathartic, they are insufficient.
All such activities must be followed with action.

Enough said.

10. THESE VOICES IN MY HEAD

"I remained too much time in my head and
ended up losing my mind"
—Edgar Allen Poe

The things you tell yourself can really mess you up. Some of us defeat ourselves even before the challenges present themselves. Poe had a stark and melancholy way of expressing himself and the opening quote is symptomatic of that. His body of work is also indicative of a reflective soul often in conflict with itself.

In the midst of this conflict lies the very human experience that is the internal battle between the forces of good and the forces of evil. These forces are the basis of the conversations we have with ourselves as we seek to attain inner peace and a degree of happiness. These are the voices in our heads and if you personalise it: these voices in my head.

These voices represent the limiting beliefs, cultural baggage, self-doubt, religious dogma, socialised propaganda and other (let's say) stuff that we carry in our conscious and subconscious minds all day, every day and all the time. While your spirit carries this load you still have visions of things you want to do in your life.

The most basic obstacle to doing what you want to do in your life is the routine of everyday life.

It's difficult to prioritise the time to pursue a great business idea when you have other things that must be done.

Things or routines like household chores, childrearing, weekly shopping, paying utility bills, parent-teacher meetings, spending time with people you don't like, dreaming of winning the lottery, attending a class you dislike, going to a job you hate etc.

Daily routines are good for self-discipline.

Daily routines that sap our energy over the years can take us away from any desire to improve ourselves.

It is quite understandable to focus on raising a family and putting the ambitions of loved ones above our own.

As a matter of fact, it is respectable, noble and honourable to do so. Yet the question beckons as to what are you doing for yourself in preparation for the time when the family is grown and everyone around you is fulfilling their potential? Let us approach this from another perspective in an attempt to avoid unnecessary offense.

Family is the cornerstone of any civilised society. We need this intimate social setting to nurture our development. Please accept that you also deserve some nurturing as you make your major contribution within the family dynamic.

Remember that you also have deeply passionate ambitions and deserve personal fulfilment. It is so easy to become defined by our roles e.g. husband, helper, son, carer, wife, daughter, eldest sibling, community leader, nurturer et al. especially when people primarily relate to us according to these unofficial job specifications.

You gather by now that examples help to support some of the perspectives shared in this book so, true to form, here's another practical example:

You need a baby sitter so; you ask your mother because she's never busy anyway and she'll want to see the children. The thought that she may have a life of her own with a pre-arranged schedule doesn't even enter your mind because you relate to her in the capacity of mother/grandmother not woman with a hobby or time to pursue her long abandoned interests after raising you.
Sensitive example but just follow the reasoning.

There is the need for the duality of mutual consideration. There is something special in thinking of someone else and that someone else thinking of you.
There is beauty in having even a modicum of empathy and it's joyful when someone just gets where you are coming from.

You are less likely to take advantage of someone's kindness when you truly value the fact that they are always kind to you. Let's return to the granny babysitting example above.

Knowing that your mother will babysit doesn't mean you always ask. Equally, knowing that you will always be asked doesn't mean you (the grandmother) must always be available.

Listening, then submitting, to the voice you hear in your head saying 'no not this time' can be hard but it's also necessary.

The different energies that come with aspects of our character often speak to us in specific voices at the right time. We are not referring to being bipolar or any other psychiatric diagnosis.
We are literally discussing the way you talk to yourself, the internal voices you hear in those quiet moments, the opposing voices that argue in your head over certain decisions.

Reading this right now and hearing it in your mind may sound strange but you know exactly what I am talking about. How come? Because you experience it. Now here's another scenario regarding the duality of mutual consideration (the first one was the babysitting example):

Your friend comes to you with the same issue and you give the same solution-based advice for six months. If your friend insists on moaning about the same situation whilst refusing to take action to change things, then there comes a point when you must stop allowing your friend to burden you with it.

The giver gives as long as the taker takes, and the taker takes as long as the giver gives. Sometimes you have to decline when something is requested from you and sometimes you simply need to stop asking for that which you should provide for yourself.

The duality of mutual consideration creates a healthy balance in our relationships. We all know people who simply don't have the heart to say no.

They regularly give of themselves to others. The duality of mutual consideration suggests that we must not over step the mark by taking their kindness for granted.

Self- empowerment is an on-going process:

A continuum of evolution.

An opportunity to identify, develop and monetise your skill sets.

The powerful way you discipline your mind to impact your actions.

Your commitment to self-empowerment is done alongside everything else you already do in your life. One of the aims of this book is to debunk many of the convoluted theories about how to make progress, measure success or sustain growth. We aim to demystify some negative preconceptions and present practical ways to support you in living the life you desire or always desired.

We intend to drive home the understanding that all you need to be successful is already within you. We will provide some tools to help you extract more of your valuable essence, so you can then confidently share it with the universe.
Sharing who you are requires knowledge of self. It's about knowledge of self, God and others.
It requires personal analysis. Please develop the willingness to engage with methodologies that improve and support your life journey to be the best version of yourself. It starts with you.

Life is full of challenges and triumphs. Life is filled with up and downs. Life has highs and lows. There are hills and valleys.
Comparing your life with anyone else's does not change the fact that your life is what it is right now even though you may hear these voices from time to time.

Blaming your childhood or dwelling on past misfortunes may comfort you emotionally but it won't change your current reality.

Painful circumstances can lead you to take legal or illegal drugs, have suicidal thoughts or dwell in depressive states of mind to ease the pain (as discussed in Chapter 7). Remember that those same painful circumstances can drive you to achieve phenomenal things.

Be brave enough to get a grip on yourself before you wreck yourself. I know it's hard but what option do you have? Shake off the negative vibes and realign your spirit. You have mighty works to do.

How you see yourself and the mindset you have about your circumstances will directly affect the way you function.

This is the moment to fix up and handle your business.

This is the moment to 'sing a different sankey' (develop another narrative), create a paradigm shift and speak to yourself more affirmatively. Reinforce positive mantras through prayer, chanting, affirmations and meditation.

Challenge the voices in your head with critical thinking. Surround yourself with people who get things done rather than those who talk about what they plan to do — one day.

You can talk yourself into failure and this is a silent killer of your ambitions. The enemy within can defeat you even before the enemies without take aim at disrupting your life plans.

I contemplate whether some people actually sabotage their own growth by filling themselves with every internal excuse as to why they are non-productive. Such unbridled self-sabotoge is done without ever accepting the role they played in their own visionary demise.

It was always someone else's fault but never their own.

This chapter is a clarion call to check how you speak with yourself because this will manifest in how you show up in this life and the way you function in all your relationships.

It will also have an impact on the rate of progress you make each day

Consider yourself and equally consider the manner with which you deal with others in whatever capacity. We tend to prejudge from a place of subjectivity, so we see things a certain way because our first frame of reference is our own experience.

I see things a certain way primarily due to how and where I was raised, plus my life experience to date. If your view is coloured by negative preconceptions, it will tarnish your ability to attain a higher level of thinking and the same applies to me.

The more such levels of toxic thought interact, the more likely they are to cause mayhem and spread counter productivity in the conversations we have in the privacy of our minds.

The voices in our heads are powerful. We must be aware of their influence and guide them aright. Have a few thoughts with yourself about what you've read while I express a few more contemplations to wrap up this chapter.

Reflection is a useful tool for growth whether it's on an individual level or part of an organisational structure. Looking back is as valuable as looking forward in the present moment.

Due to the pervasive nature of social media, we hear many stories of millionaires who 'came from nothing'. These stories are prevalent in most cultures so you either know of one or will read about one in your lifetime. Stories of people who overcome seemingly insurmountable odds to become leaders in their professions are equally prevalent.

As you admire these people, do you ever pause to think about your story or listen to the voices in your head that are encouraging you to do your thing? What's really stopping you from doing what you feel you can do? Why haven't you taken that next step in upscaling your business? When will you pursue that interest you've had all these years?

The answer has to do with these voices in your head. Mind is not brain and brain is not mind.

The reference to 'voices in my head' is the use of simple vocabulary referring to the things I say to myself and, since we are in conversation and contemplation, the things you say to yourself.

The answer has to do with these voices in your head.

We could get all fancy and wax lyrical about the subconscious mind then approach this subject from a more psychological perspective or even engage in established schools of thought to validate our discourse but that, dear reader, would be an intellectual distraction.

I'm choosing to ignore that voice in my head.

11. INTERLUDE

This is an inspirational interlude before you read the last chapter. It's a confluence of concepts to contemplate.

Your body only houses your spirit for a time. It is an unavoidable reality that we shall all transcend this life. The great impact of your ideas and the fond memories you create will live long after you physically leave this planet.

An idea whose time has come is one of the most powerful manifestations in this universe. Your life achievements will bear witness to the expression of your truth.

Standing in your truth means understanding then defining who you are. This knowledge of self enables you to walk the planet with dignity, confidence and power. You will think over an idea then act according to your decision.

Be and it is.

Keep an open mind, experience life and love yourself. Your beauty is your beauty. Read the full context of controversial speeches, go to the original source of social media soundbites and respect life choices that you may not co-sign.

Filter what your mind is seeing and never stop learning.

11. ABOUT DIVERSITY

A fascinating aspect of residing in the Western Hemisphere is that you are exposed to all manner of people, perspectives and possibilities.

Intellectualising about the notion of diversity is different from living amongst people from a range of cultures. Big cities normally have an immigrant population who bring their cultural expressions from their native lands. If you are an American descendant of slavery, it is reasonable for you to see America through a different lens than a person whose lineage lies somewhere else.

Children born in a particular place are still linked to their cultural background by virtue of language, food, religion, music, prejudices, folklore and racial experiences. Place of birth may guarantee a passport with certain rights of citizenship but the impact of culture, and the powerful way it shapes individual identity, should never be underestimated.

> **"We are what we are, that's the way It's going to be"**
> **-Bob Marley, Babylon System**

Over time the impact may lessen or be expressed in less obvious ways, however, it is always there in some shape or form. Immigrants have their culture that they adapt or flexibly apply in order to survive in foreign countries. History and empirical data support this observation anywhere on our globe. The immigrant example is fairly obvious so let us examine diversity from two more nuanced perspectives: Individual Cognisance and Tribal Connections.

INDIVIDUAL COGNISANCE.

There has never been and will never be anyone in the world like you. Science verifies this and so does critical thinking. Being unique means you have something special that no one else has. You alone were blessed with the gift you have to share in this universe.

Your life has purpose and always had a purpose. You overcame the hostile environment of your mother's womb to experience your date of birth. A particular sperm obliterated all the other spermatic competitors to pierce that egg and develop into you.

So you are born unlike anyone else, yet society wants you to always 'be like everyone else'. You are expected to 'just fit in', 'do what is expected of you' and 'be normal' or 'not standout'.

The extent to which we blindly conform to the status quo is the degree to which we kill parts of our soul. We pay heavy prices throughout our lives by trying to be other than our true selves. Not being you comes with a price tag that keeps demanding payment.

Family backgrounds, how we were raised and societal expectations can weaken our willingness to stand out and be who we know we truly are deep inside.

Developing the confidence to live according to your core values is a struggle. It's hard because sometimes life just forces us to think that there is no way out of our present conditions.
It's difficult because you will be ostracised from people who do not want you to change.

Emotional parasites have skillful ways of making you feel guilty for engaging in personal empowerment.
Friends and family may become bellicose as they realise that you are starting to change for the better. Close associates may want you to keep doing the same foolishness you've always done with them. Your significant other may tell you there is no way out from the mess you have created.

There is always a way out.
It starts with a new way of thinking.
Thought shapes matter.

Our thinking has a direct impact on how we act as human beings. People think differently. It could even be argued that some people do not seem to ever think. How we view or perceive a problem will affect how we handle it.

What we think about any given situation instructs the path we take to positively remedy or negatively inflame whatever we are facing.

The solution may come in very small steps that seem negligible in the grand scheme of things. That's fine because with each small step you are no longer where you were before. You have moved from where you were to a different and better place in your mind.

We act as we think. A proactive mindset will result in more progressive actions that in turn shape our reality for the better. Your way of assessing a situation may be the opposite of how I assess it. We may come to the same conclusion from opposing perspectives. You may have a better solution to an issue that I blindly approached in a tried and tested manner.

There is a Jamaican saying that 'two heads are better than one'. It is not to be taken literally. This metaphor alludes to the value of diversity in that two (or more) persons working together are more likely to solve a problem than a person working alone. Individuals bring a unique awareness or body of knowledge that better equips them to contribute to the ultimate solution.

Being transformed through the renewal of your mind heightens your ability to think more critically (especially when problems occur).

QUESTION: How can I change my thinking when problems occur?

ANSWER: Shut up, be quiet and take 8 deep breaths on the spot. This gives you time to immediately slow down before you allow your ego to let you do something stupid.

Sleep on it so you can be blessed with a fresh perspective after a good night's slumber. Look at the bigger picture by thinking of those who will be affected by how you decide to handle this problem.

Carry a picture of someone you love then look at

that picture in the moment of crisis. The warm feelings that you get from that picture will alter your state of mind, which is a good thing under the circumstances.

You can also say a quick prayer, count to 10, hum your favourite song, read a scripture, think of someone you love or chant: Nam Myoho Renge Kyo.

Understanding and accepting you are different is an excellent starting point in your journey of individual cognisance. Embracing the power in your difference is the precursor to living successfully and monetizing your skills, your gifts and your talents.

It's ok to be you.
It is a blessing to be you.

All you should truly aim to be is yourself. Nobody can be you but you. This naturally powerful advantage of being so individual must be celebrated, cultivated and nourished as often as possible. This awareness is the key to unlocking your successful life. There will be compromises to be made and challenges to face as you progress towards the essence of who you are. We live with other people on this planet so there are laws and social rules of engagement to observe. Individual cognisance means you shine your light in the darkness of a world that encourages you to hide your magnificence.

Individual cognisance edifies your spirit to cultivate all the visions you see in your mind.

Individual cognisance allows each of us to cherish the inner strength necessary to function in alignment with our purpose, gift or higher calling. Your consciousness is dynamic. Be aware of the divinity within.

Realize the value and magnificence of the only universe. The only universe is the one inside you. You are in a stronger position for family, national and global impact through practicing individual cognisance – the consciousness that develops from engaging in thoughts, actions and strategies for personal empowerment.

As you reap the benefits of this process you will gravitate towards people who reflect similar growth. You are able to collaborate with others from a position of strength because you know your worth both creatively and financially. You function from a place of abundance knowing that your talent is beyond boundaries

You will continue to develop your skillsets as you appreciate how good you are at what you do and as you continue to master your craft. We shall segue into the other nuanced perspective as we contemplate the subject of diversity.

TRIBAL CONNECTIONS.
It is natural to gravitate towards people, things and circumstances that resonate with you.
There is comfort in the familiar and security in that which we are used to. Prejudging is also natural because we are all impacted by the factors that influence us.
We see the world through our lenses of individual experiences.

The problem arises when we seek to impose our prejudgments upon others. This is both arrogant and disrespectful because it disregards the fact that they too see the world through their individual experiences.

We must seek to embrace diverse perspectives even as we work for the common good.

The magnetism of likeminded people is powerful. This power is elevated when the intentions are positive, as history is replete with examples of what happens when people collaborate for evil.

People form tribes as an organic outgrowth of commonality. People who have similar interests, views, eating habits and ways of life are more likely to come together than those who do not share such interests.

Tribes share values that their members understand and generally abide by. You feel special because this is your tribe so your membership carries an aura of exclusivity about it.

Branding makes consumers feel special by association in the similar way that taking a picture with someone you admire makes you feel important.

A well-made handbag is a well-made handbag and a properly designed pair of sneakers is a properly designed pair of sneakers. Handbags and footwear are distinguished by how they make the consumer feel by aligning themselves with the values that the makers espouse through branding.

Advertising creates the desire within us to purchase a given product or service. We are stimulated to buy because of the perceived value we associate with said product or service.

We want to be part of this tribal connection. This value of belonging to a group is also evident in religious beliefs, music preferences, academic circles, contemporary style and many other walks of life. It is natural to want to be with people with whom you have things in common.
People striving to be themselves are also a tribe.

A tribe may be explained by way of the ancient Roman definition rooted in the Latin word 'tribus' denoting division in the state. A tribe may also be seen as a description of the diverse cultures encountered through European exploration. Neither of the aforementioned definitions applies in this context.

A tribe is to be contextually understood as a human social group and a tribal connection is the relationship between these associated or linked people. Being clear about who you are increases your tendency to form relationships (connections) with people who have things in common with you and those who enhance your life (tribe).
Social media groups are tribal connections.
Lobbying groups are tribal connections.
My fellow coffee lovers are tribal connections.
Military units are tribal connections.
Book clubs are tribal connections.

We achieve more together so it is useful to find your tribe and enjoy another level of fulfillment in your life.

There is much focus on diversity and inclusion at the time of writing. It appears well intended and in many instances laws have been passed with the aim of leveling the playing field in areas where there is evident disparity.

All such efforts are to be rightfully acknowledged and duly applauded. If history has taught us anything, it is that neither lip service nor laws can change people's attitudes.

You must also actively assert your individuality through self-respect and the pursuit of personal empowerment in order to express your higher consciousness in this lifetime.

Embrace all of the affirming changes around you and do your part to further enhance the changes that manifest around you.

Be cognisant of your individuality and then associate with your tribe whilst scaling even greater heights in the unique tapestry of your life.

Command respect for who you are. Command rather than beg. Command it by living according to your core values however strange they may initially appear to others. This is the essence of diversity: the understanding that uniquely different approaches serve as valuable contributors in the achievement of a particular vision and a better world.

As we appreciate our individual uniqueness and celebrate with our tribes, it is possible to drown in the sea of cross sectionalism. The tributaries of our differences that make up diversity often serve as dams leading into a river flowing in the direction of justice for all under every circumstance and in in all conditions. While justice for all is the ideal, it is also utopian and individually or tribally unrealistic.

We cannot be all things to all people at all times without some things and some people coming up short or being ignored some of the time.

A balloon will surely burst when filled with too much air. Excessive cross sectionalism involves trying to link many things under one umbrella without regard for factors that distinguish them. Placing many ingredients in a pot doth not an excellent gumbo make.

One must be clear about the amount, type and nature of ingredients used before they are put in the pot to get the uniquely delicious result that is a gumbo. It may appear haphazard to the untrained eye but it is far from that.

It is wise to respect that there are levels of understanding when dealing with diversity and inclusion. There is no one-size-fits-all-approach.

An aspect of diversity includes respecting inherent differences.
It also includes acknowledging that unique approaches bring perspectives that are often more effective than everyone trying the same approach.

"You must learn to love to be different.
Don't follow the herd"
-George Attah Eggay

From the life wisdom of a great Ghanaian and elevated thinker as told to his son, George-Jalal E. Muhammad.

13. REFLECTIONS

Thank you for keeping an open mind as you read my perspectives and contemplations on the subjects in each chapter.

Please remember to trust your gut, act on your visions and continue to expand your mind from a position of knowledge and fact rather than misinformation and emotion.

The secret to success is aligning your spirit with your purpose, then taking consistent and focused actions. Much of this is determined by how you think and the way you use your skillsets.

Nature has laws in the similar way that your body systems function according to their purpose. Developing efficient and consistent rituals, habits, procedures and systems should be a natural part of your life.

You are encouraged to explore the perspectives that appeal to you and apply them in your life.

This book was written to help you to productively navigate your journey through life.

*My previous book **Empower Yourself To Succeed** was only written because Haneefah Muhammad had the vision, believed in the concept, supported the artistic process and critiqued the content. My name is on the cover, but the real drive and creatively intelligent input came from this beneficent, intuitive, virtuous and supremely talented second self of Allah. I owe her an eternal debt of gratitude, reverence and appreciation.*

Let me close with this.

You are god having a human experience in this lifetime. It all comes down to that dash between birth and your spiritual transition. Use your time productively and give thanks for all the genuine love and support you receive.

Leave your mark in this universe because you are the living memory of future ancestors.

Love with all your soul.
Live with purpose.
Create a powerful legacy.

Printed in Great Britain
by Amazon

38498639R00079